Social Media and the
Search for Truth

Table of Contents

The problem with internet quotes is that you can't always depend on their accuracy

— Abraham Lincoln

Chapter 1. Introduction

In light of the ever-evolving digital landscape, our Special Report dives into an intricate paradox of our time: Social Media and the Search for Truth. With a bombardment of information every click of the way, discerning facts from fiction can seem like finding a needle in the proverbial haystack. Let us accompany you on a compelling journey to uncover the complex relationship between truth and untruth, ultimately empowering you with informed perspectives and resilience in the age of misinformation. Playfully illustrated yet rooted in profound insights, this report will prove to be an invaluable guide for digital explorers. Buckle up, because this Special Report promises to be as fascinating as it is essential, injecting both cheerfulness and clarity into a cloudy digital world. A must-have for everyone navigating the meandering paths of social media today—because nothing reveals truth like knowledge. Order your copy today, and let's start this compelling expedition together!

Chapter 2. Setting the Stage: The Rise of Social Media

The genesis of human communication can be traced back thousands of years ago, to the utilization of primitive symbols and signs. However, the recent evolution towards the realm of social media can incontrovertibly be marked as a significantly transformative shift in the way we communicate, learn, interact, and even perceive the world.

2.1. The Dawn of Social Media

The nascence of twenty-first century brought forth an era of digital revolution that undoubtedly swept the world off its feet. Dial-up modems were replaced with broadband internet, slothful desktops with swift laptops, and by mid 2000s, the internet landscape transitioned from being nothing more than static weblogs to dynamically interactive platforms, burgeoning with content shared by millions of ordinary users just like you and me. This was the onset of social media - an epoch making phenomenon that metamorphosed our ability to communicate, connect and create.

2.2. The Turning Point: From Personal Diaries to Global Networks

In July 2003, a platform called Myspace was launched, providing users with the novel opportunity to create custom profiles, blog about their interests, share photos and videos, and in the process, begin shaping their digital personas. A few months later, Mark Zuckerberg and his Harvard classmates introduced TheFacebook, which would be later renamed to Facebook. Its meteoric rise can be attributed to its user-oriented model that focused on fostering connections and maintaining relationships.

Shortly thereafter, Twitter set the stage for sharing ideas in bite-sized chunks. LinkedIn served the professional networking segment, and Instagram transformed visual sharing by leveraging the power of photographs. Then came YouTube, revolutionizing video content. These platforms, among many others, blossomed into global networks, impacting lives on an unparalleled scale.

2.3. A Shift in Power Dynamics: From Gatekeepers to Grassroots

Before the advent of social media, big conglomerates tightly controlled information production and dissemination, thereby shaping public opinion. Newspapers, radio and television broadcasts were the primary source of news. The hierarchical one-way flow of information put the masses at the receiving end with limited access to voice their opinions.

The advent of social media altered this power structure dramatically. With new media, the power was diffused, and every user was bestowed the ability to share their perspective with the world. This shift from gatekeepers to grassroots led to an outburst of user-generated content, democratising information and potentially enhancing free speech.

2.4. The Culture of Sharing and Creating

Social media encouraged a culture of sharing, driving people to express their opinions, ideas, creativity, and even mundane daily routines. With a potential audience of millions, if not billions, users became both consumers and generators of content. This perpetuated a cycle of creation and consumption which in turn cemented social media's place in our everyday lives.

2.5. The Global Village Theory and Social Media

Marshall McLuhan's 'Global Village' theory perfectly encapsulates the impact of social media on society. He theorized that technology, especially electronic media, would lead to integration and interdependence on a global scale, creating a 'global village'. We can observe this today in how social media allows us to connect with anyone, anywhere, transcending geographical barriers.

In conclusion, the dawn and rise of social media have left an indelible mark on humanity by revolutionizing communication norms and enhancing global connectivity. This journey from personal diaries to global networks, where the balance of power shifted from gatekeepers to grassroots, cultivated a novel culture of sharing and creating under the aegis of the Global Village Theory. As we move forward, it is essential to acknowledge and appreciate the scale of transformation driven by social media while vigilantly navigating its future trajectories.

Chapter 3. Understanding the Magnitude: Social Media Influence

Social media platforms, an offshoot of the digital revolution, have reshaped the traditional landscape of communication. From a past characterized by linear, one-to-one communication methodologies, we've pivoted reluctantly yet inexorably towards a present tattooed with intricate social structures constructed on these digital platforms. The impacts are all-encompassing. They resonate in the crux of our societies and, inevitably, influence our perception of the world.

3.1. The Face of Influence: Understanding Its Scope

To comprehend the extent of social media influence, we must first unpack the concept of 'influence.' In essence, influence refers to a power or capacity to be a compelling force on the actions, behavior, and opinions of others. Concurrently, social media platforms act as these influence-touting vehicles, ever-changing entities triggering these mechanisms of influence. This is primarily due to their architecture, which encourages user engagement, interaction and the free flow of information harmoniously.

Social media statistics reflect this startling reality with accuracy. As of 2022, there are 4.48 billion social media users worldwide, equating to approximately 57% of the global population. This statistic alone is indicative of the sheer magnitude of the potential influence that these platforms exercise. A pronounced shift has hence been seen in how people consume media,

with traditional sources rapidly being supplaced by
social media feeds.

3.2. The Mechanisms of Influence: Persuasive Power of Social Media

Social media platforms hold a persuasive power that extends through their creation and circulation of content. The manner of such circulation employs intricate algorithms often based on individual user behavior. These algorithms dictate the flow of information that users receive, creating what is often referred to as 'Filter Bubbles' or 'Echo Chambers.'

Filter bubbles are defined as the intellectual isolation that can occur when websites make use of algorithms to predict and subsequently show users what they want to see, thereby tailoring the perspective of the worldly discourse presented to them. The personalization of these digital spaces reduces exposure to conflicting viewpoints, reinforcing users' current beliefs, attitudes, or biases. Echo chambers, an offshoot of this phenomenon, refer to situations where individuals are exposed only to opinions that echo and reinforce their own.

These phenomena inculcate certain beliefs in users, often blurring the line between reality and perception, to manipulate them into gravitating towards certain ideological, political, or commercial leanings. For instance, advertising on social media, an industry worth billions, capitalizes on these mechanisms for targeted campaigns.

3.3. Bottom-up Influence: User Generated Content

The imposition of influence does not remain strictly top-down in the realm of social media. A significant segment of its influence emanates from the bottom-up end of the spectrum, where users generate their content and influence their followers.

Such bottom-up influence comes in various forms - impassioned citizen journalism, individual influencers with significant followers, or viral trends that circulate among the users. These elements can have a profound impact, steering public discourse in various directions. For instance, the Arab Spring, catalyzed by the free flow of communication over social media among laypeople, illustrates this power vividly.

It is important to mention that this user-generated influence is not always benign. It can foster the proliferation of misinformation, digital bullying, and hate speech, further highlighting the complexity of social media's influence.

3.4. The Silent Sentinel: Privacy and Surveillance

With every scroll, click, like, or share, users contribute to the digital datascape that fuels these platforms' ubiquitous influence. This vast sea of data, analyzed, and interpreted through advanced machine learning and AI algorithms, enables social media platforms to predict, infer, and ultimately influence user behavior significantly.

This silent sentinel of surveillance raises concerns regarding privacy and the ethical boundaries of such data usage. Yet, in an implicit transaction, users continue to trade their privacy for the convenience and connection that these platforms provide, often unaware of the pervasive influence they imbibe in the process.

This chapter may paint a somewhat disconcerting picture of the mammoth influence of social media. However, an understanding of the magnitude and mechanisms of social media influence is the first step towards envisaging strategies to mitigate its negative consequences and harness its positive potential. As we navigate through this vast digital landscape, we must keep a firm hand on the tiller of discernment and skepticism, ensuring that we remain the directors. It's up to us to determine whether social media is the tool or master in this digital dialogue. The journey of understanding that starts now will indeed prove instrumental for the chapters ahead.

Chapter 4. Bridging the Gap: Social Media & Real Life

Social media platform X—that will be our starting point. Now, imagine waking up to instantly dive into logging into platform X, scrolling through updates and posts with half-closed eyes, and ending the day with a final check of the latest happenings. Sounds pretty straightforward, right? However, the inescapable question that arises is: how much does this virtual reality overlap with our actual reality—our real lives? The shadows of our digital personas have humbly intertwined themselves into our existence, making this question not just a philosophical inquiry, but a much-needed exploration of our current lives. This chapter seeks to bridge the gap between the lavishly constructed interfaces of social media platforms and the reality of lives outside the screens.

4.1. The Mirror Effect

Imagine walking into a hall of mirrors, with each reflecting a portion of who you really are, multiplied and distorted. That's precisely the spectacle social media often presents. Each post, each like, each share, makes up parts of our digital mirror—continually multiplying, replicating, and sometimes distorting our real selves. We adopt multiple identities, intersecting, overlapping, challenging and sometimes even contradicting who we are in reality. This 'Mirror Effect' is an essential element that bridges the reality of our lives and our social media presence.

4.2. The Metrics of Validation

Moreover, given the element of instant gratification that accompanies social media use, it is only natural for us to fall into the quantification trap—where likes, shares, and comments become cardinal indicators of self-worth and validation. This aforementioned 'Metrics of Validation' forms a significant part of the bridge between real life and social media. It's a conundrum as life lends no such metrics—no quantifiable means to ascertain our individual worth. Consequently, the real and digital blend, leaving many in the paradoxical position of living a life parallelly in cyberspace and real-time, the former incessantly influencing the perception of the latter.

4.3. Digital Self versus Real Self

Indeed, the lines between our online personas and real selves have blurred considerably. Some argue that our digital self is often an escape—an ideal version of ourselves or who we'd like to be. If so, is the authenticity we seek merely an illusion? This 'Digital Self versus Real Self' paradox poses a significant dilemma in bridging the reality of everyday life and our virtual existence. Cultural, social, and individual pressures often steer us to present ourselves in a particular way, shaping our digital image into a distinct entity—a form that technically exists in parallel to our real selves.

4.4. Digital Activism and Real-world Impact

Of course, not everything that happens online stays on the internet. The rise of digital activism is a perfect example of how actions on social media affect real-world change. Movements like #BlackLivesMatter have swept across platforms, mobilizing millions, and succeeding in forcing substantial changes in the real world. Thus, 'Digital Activism and Real-world Impact' are inseparable in our modern milieu—forming a substantial part of the bridge between social media and real life.

As we dive deeper into the complexities of our digital and physical personas, the bridge connecting social media with real life becomes more apparent. Extricating ourselves entirely from the digital sphere is not an option in our modern world. However, we can, and must, ensure that the bridge between our real life and virtual presence is constantly scrutinized. This process would help prevent a total eclipse of our realities by our digital selves, thus preserving the essence of truth—the veritable core of our lives. The upcoming sections will further dissect our relationship with social media—enabling us to glimpse the discipline required to handle these powerful tools wisely, accurately gauge the reach and limitations of such platforms, and guide our journey through the endless maze of information and misinformation prevalent in the digital age.

Overall, bridging the gap between social media and real life involves a multifaceted approach to understand the role digital platforms play in our everyday lives. With that understanding, we can hope to shed light on the complexities, paradoxes and potential solutions in this evolving digital landscape. Only through such in-depth exploration can we hope to uncover the truth, and perhaps, paradoxically, even find solace in the complexity of our digital lives.

Chapter 5. The Paradox: Navigating the Information Overload

The digital age, without a doubt, ushers us into an era of unprecedented access to an astoundingly vast and ceaselessly growing reservoir of information. This expansion in information availability carries a paradoxically puzzling dilemma: rather than facilitating clarity, the information overload on social media platforms often births confusion, making it ever more challenging to delineate factual truth.

5.1. Unfolding the Paradox

The said paradox stems from the fact that social media platforms, initially designed as mere communication tools, swiftly swelled into massive distribution networks for information of all sort—rigorous journalism, personal opinions, advertisements, memes, and unfortunately, misinformation. With an innumerable number of data bits being shared and consumed every second, discerning accurate, relevant, and crucial information becomes a Daedalian task for the average social media consumer.

The paradox of information overload begins to unfurl itself when one starts to decipher that the more information provided, rather than enhancing our understanding or perspective, oftenly fetishizes confusion, inaccuracy, and intellectual fatigue. This is a repercussion resulting from our cognitive unit's inability to effectively process and evaluate information exceeding its limit.

5.2. Information Illiteracy: A Contributing Factor

The essence of the problem lies with what is termed "information literacy" or, more accurately, the lack thereof. It is the ability to discern, analyze, and evaluate data that is relevant and reliable from an ocean of information, which is becoming alarmingly scarce in the digital era. With several amplified voices vying for attention, the limited user attention span often falls prey to the loudest, most sensational voices, not always quality or credibility.

Conversely, in an attempt to engage and retain users on their platforms, algorithmic systems of social media platforms often exhibit a behavioral tendency dissected as 'filter bubbles' or 'echo chambers'. This essentially means that individuals are predominantly exposed to information that aligns with their existing beliefs, ideologies, or preferences, reducing the chance encounter with differing perspectives and therewith possibly nurturing an intellectual stagnancy.

5.3. Misinterpretation of Information: A Silent Culprit

Another equally culpable aspect is the tendency of users to misinterpret, miscontextualize, or misaccount for the information they encounter. This could be due to an inherent cognitive bias or through external manipulation of the presented information. Additionally, given the brevity-demanding nature of social media, the need for nuance and context may often be discarded, making room for over-simplifications, misconceptions, and unfounded speculations.

5.4. Thinking Fast and Slow: The Psychology Behind Information Overload

Understanding this paradox necessitates delving into the realm of psychology—specifically cognitive psychology. In his book "Thinking, Fast and Slow", Nobel laureate Daniel Kahneman introduces the concepts of System 1 and System 2 thinking. System 1 represents an automatic, quick and frequent mode of thinking, often influenced by biases, and does more harm than good when discerning nuanced information. Conversely, System 2 is effortful, logical, slow, and calculative, conducive to discerning facts from fiction but tiring when the information flow is too abundant. The vast majority of digital information consumption occurs under System 1 thinking owing to the colossal amount of data being encountered. This fosters a fertile ground for misinformation to thrive.

5.5. Mitigation Measures: In Search of A Panacea

One may argue that the solution against this is developing a suite of cognitive tools and literacies allowing us to smartly navigate the complex digital landscape. This includes but is not limited to: critical thinking, digital literacy, and emotional intelligence.

However, a noteworthy part of the responsibility also rests on the architects of these social media platforms, to make algorithmic adjustments ensuring the distribution of credible, diverse, and valuable information. Policy revisions, transparency in algorithmic processes, and cooperation in global regulations could be few steps towards addressing the information overload paradox.

Though certainly no panacea exists for this multifaceted alpha-problem of the digital age, a well-rounded, multi-stakeholder approach seems the most promising.

5.6. Conclusion: Understanding is The First Step

Information overload on social media is a paradox that calls for subjective discernment and objective screening. While we grapple to identify and implement the best solutions, a critical first step is to understand the paradox itself. By acknowledging the issue and comprehending its implications, we carve a path towards calibrating our attitudes, responses, and systems to navigate the digital information influx more efficaciously.

In the grand scheme of things, social media is a relatively novel phenomenon, and this paradox of information overload is one we have recognized only recently. As our understanding of these platforms grows, so too will our ability to combat the challenges they present, framing them as tools for enlightenment rather than sources of confusion. This is the turning point where the Paradox starts to lose its power, and the field of objective truth commences its ascension.

Thus, we end this chapter with the hope that a conscious and collective effort by individuals, technologists, academicians, and policymakers may progressively unravel this paradox, steering us closer to the search of truth in the virtually noisy, yet incredibly potent, world of social media.

Chapter 6. Illusion vs Reality: The Celebration of Half-truths

In the digital realm of social media, nestled amidst the pet videos, the memes, and the show-off vacation photos, there lies a cloak and dagger dichotomy between illusion and reality - often presenting itself as a hoard of half-truths, partial narratives, or disguised lies. This chapter aims to unravel the essence of this dichotomy, to dissect the elements that give birth to this murky environment, and to illustrate the consequences it invokes.

6.1. The Delicate Lacework of Half-truths

Deconstructing half-truths requires an understanding of their nature. A half-truth is a deceptive statement, which includes some element of truth but misses out the entire context or utilizes clever language to distort the reality. The danger lies not in the lie itself, but the sprinkle of veracity that makes it enticing and believable. Social media, given its vastness and speed, serve as an effective vehicle for the spread of these malformations of information. The enticing allure of the "like" button, the instantaneous gratification acquired from "shares", and the digital hierarchy established by "followers" have exacerbated the situation, prompting even the most unsuspecting users to occasionally indulge in half-truths.

6.2. Reality Distortion: From Photo Filters to Filter Bubbles

The celebration of half-truths permeates beyond contentious topics and into the domain of self-representation. Instagram's X-Pro II or Snapchat's beloved dog filter might seem harmless, but they contribute to a culture of reality distortion, offering a glossy, doctored reality that often feels unattainable in offline life. Simultaneously, the workings of algorithms generate filter bubbles that amplify our existing viewpoints, compromising our ability to access objective truth.

6.3. The Chronicles of Misinformation

Misinformation exploits our vulnerabilities, primarily our cognitive biases, and leaps across social networks at a speed that truth often struggles to match. Be it the sensational headlines or conspiracy theories, their proliferation is fueled by the potent combination of confirmation bias and the illusion-of-truth effect. Misinformation can also snowball into larger issues such as the spread of harmful propaganda or public health crises, thereby underscoring the serious implications of these half-truths.

6.4. The Unseen Costs of Half-truths

The perpetuation of half-truths triggers a domino effect with far-reaching impacts. Trust erodes, skepticism grows, and people start living in divergent realities, dissected along their belief systems. Panic induced buying during a pandemic or sharp shifts in stock market indices based on baseless rumors are stark examples of how large-scale behavioral changes can be traced back to a small tweet or a misleading Facebook post.

6.5. Navigating the Mirage: Tools and Tactics

Identification and correction of half-truths demand a nuanced approach, including media literacy, critical thinking, and an understanding of cognitive biases. Algorithmic efforts, like Facebook's fact-check mechanisms, and third-party fact-checking outlets, like Snopes or FactCheck.org, are proving beneficial. Individuals are also resorting to slow-thinking, questioning sources, and cross-verification to stand against the tide of misinformation.

Social media, much like an elephant, exhibits different facets depending upon where one stands. While these platforms have undoubtedly democratized information and made global communication easier, they have also become a breeding ground for partial truths. The call of the hour is to develop a comprehensive understanding of this complexity and to foster diligence in engaging with social media. Remember, sometimes the most enthralling stories on these platforms are indeed just that – stories.

Chapter 7. The Battle Within: Cognitive Biases and the Spread of Misinformation

The examination of the twinned roles of social media and misinformation would miss the mark significantly without the exploration of another contributing factor – cognitive biases. A cognitive bias refers to a systematic error in thinking, affecting the judgements and decisions that people make. What makes these biases particularly troubling in the context of social media, is their often unseen yet profound influence on the spread of misinformation.

7.1. A Foray into the Functionality of Cognitive Biases

At its core, a cognitive bias serves as a mental shortcut, a heuristic allowing us to process information and make decisions swiftly amidst a sea of stimuli. Such efficiency, while laudable in numerous scenarios, often results in inadvertent errors. Errors which, in the scope of social media, can directly contribute to the circulation of misinformation.

To effectively appreciate the role of cognitive biases in spreading misinformation on social media, we must first comprehend some typical cognitive biases that tend to run rampant in such gears.

- **Confirmation bias** is probably the most recognised cognitive bias and plays a paramount role. It describes the phenomenon where people tend to search for and interpret information that confirms their pre-existing beliefs or hypotheses, whilst ignoring or the same time trivializing any contradictory information.

- **Availability heuristic** refers to our predilection to rely heavily on immediate examples that come to mind when evaluating a specific topic, concept, method or decision. In the social media context, it could mean believing a piece of news or information to be accurate just because it's widely shared or readily available.

- **Bandwagon effect** or **groupthink** is the propensity to adopt certain behaviours, beliefs or actions merely because many other individuals are doing so. It perfectly describes the scenario in which fake news could be adopted as truth just because a large group, including peers and celebrities, endorses it.

- **Anchoring bias**, otherwise known as focalism, is a psychological bias where an individual relies too heavily on an initial piece of information offered (the "anchor") to make subsequent judgments.

- **False consensus bias** or **pluralistic ignorance** refers to a cognitive bias whereby a person incorrectly believes that their views or beliefs are ordinary when that may not be the case, leading to an overconfidence in personal beliefs and their subsequent spread.

7.2. The Implication of Biases in the Misinformation Matrix

It is through these silent arbiters of thought that the diffusion of misinformation finds its footing. Take confirmation bias for instance - when fed with a misinformation that aligns with a person's beliefs, they are imminently more likely to accept and share said information, disregarding any underlying veracity.

Availability heuristic plays a particularly devastating role in scenarios where misinformation is amplified through repeated sharing, making it readily available and therefore, more believable. Combine this with the bandwagon effect, and we are left with a recipe for a misinformation wildfire, one, that once sparked, proves difficult to contain.

Anchoring bias and false consensus bias also contribute to the misinformation domino effect. Anchoring bias often leads to the propagation of first-reported, unverified pieces of information, while false consensus bias ensures an enduring commitment to misinformation based on the misguided belief that such misinformation is the general consensus.

7.3. Mitigating Cognitive Bias: An Integral Part of the Misinformation Solution

Bringing cognitive biases to light does not mean we resign ourselves to their control. In fact, the understanding thereof could serve as an integral part of our defence against misinformation. Building a cognizance and mindfulness of these biases can help prompt deeper thought, more extensive research, and greater critique of the information we encounter.

In the undertaking to counter cognitive biases, cultivation of a healthy skepticism should be nurtured. Skepticism encourages us to dig deeper into the haystack, rather than simply grazing its surface, which invariably empowers our ability to distinguish between true and false information.

Influencing more prominent social media platforms to offer and improve their digital literacy resources could aid in furthering this countermeasure. These resources may encompass guidance on how to appraise the credibility of sources, how to best scrutinize content, and strategies to keep cognitive biases in check.

To wrap up, cognitive biases tend to act as a silent conductor that directs the misinformation train on social media tracks. However, understanding and addressing these biases could, in effect, serve as an unsuspected deterrent to misinformation. By being aware of these mental shortcuts and taking off our cognitive 'blinkers', we can navigate the riddled roads of social media more consciously and more truthfully. So, the next time you ponder over the authenticity of a sensational piece of information fluttering across your screen, ponder over the biases that may be silently, yet incessantly, underpinning your judgement.

Chapter 8. Getting to The Core: The Polyhedral Truth in Social Media

In an era fraught with artificial intelligence algorithms, carefully curated content, and intricate projection of realities, we find ourselves spiraling down the wormhole of grappling with the polyhedral truth in social media. This chapter breaks down this formidable task, illuminating various dimensions of truth in the complex socio-digital universe, ultimately equipping you with skills to dissect the seemingly impenetrable layers of information we interact with.

8.1. The Multifaceted Truth in Social Media

Standing tall like a prism refracting light in multiple directions, the 'Truth' as understood within the sphere of social media is a multifaceted phenomenon. It spins an intricate web, curating a blend of reality, half-truths, and misinformation. Each online persona adds its unique shade, turning the truth into a resplendent tapestry, radiating with numerous perspectives—yet, intimidating for its vast complexity and untraceability.

8.2. Interacting with the Online Self

Cognitive psychologists highlight the prevalence of an 'online self', a virtual persona that many of us parade on social media platforms. This persona is often selectively authentic, encapsulating the highlights of our lives while leaving out the mundane realities or unattractive blemishes. The 'Truth', as seen through these meticulously curated perspectives, thus becomes tinted, embodying a partial reality that could often be mistaken for the absolute.

8.3. Biases that Lens Reality

The scene of the social media landscape is orchestrated by powerful algorithms that learn from our actions, predict our preferences, and cater results accordingly. This leads us to experience an 'online echo chamber', where we view the world through the lens of our own biases and influencing algorithms. Consequently, the interpretation of truth gets cloaked under our cognitive biases and the algorithm's predictive patterns.

8.4. Illusion of Validation

Online viewpoints that align with ours garner our attention and generally enjoy validation via likes and shares. This illusion of validation creates a conducive environment for half-truths and misinformation to proliferate, often leaving room for belief perseverance even in the face of retraction or debunking.

8.5. Understanding the Role of Deepfakes

The advent of deepfakes, artificial intelligence synthesized media, adds an especially challenging layer to deciphering truth online. These compellingly realistic images, voicing, or footage can twist reality into unrecognizable forms, making it increasingly difficult to determine the veracity of content consumed.

8.6. A Path Towards Discerning the Truth

Going forward, understanding the polyhedral truth in social media will hinge on fostering critical thinking, digital literacy, transparent algorithms, and robust fact-checking mechanisms. Knowledge of the ways in which information is skewed, hiring the services of fact-checkers, relying on multiple sources, and cultivating an open mind free of cognitive confines can be your compass while navigating through this labyrinth of truth and untruth.

8.7. Preparing for the Opaque Future

Social media is a dynamic entity, constantly evolving, shaping, and reshaping the way we interact with information. As the lines between the virtual and real world continue to blur, we need to equip ourselves to contend with this challenge that will undeniably magnify in the future. Combating the distortion of truth in the realm of social media is no longer an exclusive responsibility of fact-checkers and digital platforms but is a collective endeavor of all digital citizens.

This chapter directs us to confront the uncomfortable, enabling us to dissect, discern, and grasp the polyhedral truth in social media. It invites us to peek behind the alluring facades, scrutinize the echoed validations, strip bare the algorithmic biases, and proactively engage with information. Striving for such discernment, while daunting, is a necessary endeavor and one that holds immense potential to revolutionize the way we interact with our digital world.

Chapter 9. Countermeasures: Tracing the Authenticity of Information

In our interconnected global society, where information travels at an astonishing speed, there arises the heightened necessity of effectively identifying the genuine from the deceitful. Although it may seem like a daunting task, our chapter unfolds specific countermeasures anyone can adapt to trace the authenticity of information gleaned from social media. Nestled within the mechanics of fact-checking, AI-assisted verification tools, and the cultivation of media literacy, authenticity tracing forms the bulwark against the tide of misinformation.

9.1. Fact-Checking: Readers' Immediate Responsibility

For any individual encountering a piece of information, the initial line of defense against misinformation is fact-checking. As a practice, this anticipates a considerable level of discipline and skepticism from readers encountering any data. It's the act of pausing and not immediately sharing anything that appears even slightly dubious.

Fact-checking can involve investigating the source of the information: Is the original poster or article writer a reputable institution or individual with a proven track record of truthfulness? Furthermore, it might entail cross-referencing the data forwarded with other known sources. If the same narrative is being touted by trusted globally-established news outlets, scientific journals, or authorities in the subject matter under investigation, it lends credence to the information.

One approach is the SIFT method, comprising Stop, Investigate the source, Find better coverage, and Trace claims, quotes, and media to original context, originally proposed by Mike Caulfield in his book "Web Literacy for Student Fact-Checkers." It simplifies the process, making it more accessible for everyone to apply when encountering information that requires verification.

9.2. AI-Assisted Verification Tools

Technology, as much as it has inadvertently facilitated the spread of misinformation, can be a potent ally in counteracting it. Artificial Intelligence (AI) and Machine Learning (ML) are increasingly being used to develop verification tools for both text and images.

AI-assisted tools like bot detectors can lend a helping hand in discerning whether a user spreading particular information is actually a bot designed to proliferate misinformation. Machine Learning models can also be used to identify deepfake videos and images, or altered content designed to mislead.

Optical Character Recognition (OCR) tools can be used for verifying scanned documents while reverse image search engines like Google's can help trace the source of an image. Crowdsourced fact-checking platforms like PolitiFact and Snopes, and URL investigating tools such as NewsGuard, can be formidable assets when it comes to verifying the authenticity of information on social media. Moreover, social media platforms themselves are crafting AI-assisted fact-checking tools to provide instant validation or red-flag suspicious content.

9.3. Cultivating Media Literacy

While fact-checking and AI-assisted tools play crucial roles in fighting misinformation, these battles are only small wins in the larger war. The primal solution, one which fosters a resilient defense against the misinformation onslaught, is to cultivate media literacy.

Media literacy involves a nuanced understanding of how media works and the ability to critically analyze and comprehend various types of media communications. The capacity to discern the hidden messages, implications, and intent behind the information disseminated requires a strong foundation of media literacy.

Media literacy education encourages the development of critical thinking skills necessary to identify misinformation. It also nurtures the ability to comprehend the mechanisms employed by social media algorithms, which may perpetuate echo chambers and feed bias.

In this regard, non-profit organizations such as the Center for Media Literacy (CML) and the National Association for Media Literacy Education (NAMLE) provide comprehensive resources that foster media literacy across various age groups, from school-going children to adults.

It is through fact-checking, effective use of AI-assisted tools, and promoting media literacy that we as a global community can start to trace and validate the authenticity of information, thereby mitigating the onslaught of misinformation. The foundation of counteracting misinformation, as illustrated in this chapter, revolves around the intertwined trio of technology, a proactive populace equipped with verification tools, and the nurturing of media literacy. By embracing these countermeasures, society en masse will become better inoculated against the risk of falsehoods, thereby enhancing the prospects of information veracity in the digital age.

Chapter 10. Case Studies: Truth Quests in the Age of Social Media

In the vast, interconnected cosmos of the internet, where digital data streams intertwine, creating a robust, highly intricate network of information exchange, there are numerous narratives, real and imagined, that infiltrate our digital lives. This entangled web can, on the one hand, enrich our understanding of the world, while on the other, it can distort our sense of reality—muddying the waters between truth and untruth. With innumerable dramatic turn of events and consequential cases, let us shine a bright light onto the most significant instances that vividly illustrate our quest for truth in the age of social media.

10.1. The Mirage of Virality: The Case of the Covington Catholic Incident

On a chilly January day in 2019, a story broke across social media about an incident involving Covington Catholic High School students and a Native American elder at the Lincoln Memorial. Initial portrayals on social media suggested that the students, who were participating in the March for Life and wearing 'Make America Great Again' hats, were disrespectfully smirking at the elder Nathan Phillips, as he performed a traditional American Indian chant. These video snippets flooded various social platforms igniting a voracious digital outcry accusing the students of racism.

However, subsequent investigations and a more complete video record of the incident challenged the original narrative, painting a substantially different and far more nuanced perspective: the students were not the instigators, but rather, the recipients of heated racial slurs by a group called the Black Hebrew Israelites. This created an uproar among users, igniting a maelstrom of heated debates that lampooned mainstream media for their premature judgment and their failure to practice due diligence in dissecting this incident. This episode serves as a heartrending reminder of the potential of misinformation dispersal within the realm of social media, where fragmented or decontextualized information can rapidly spiral out of control, catalyzing often unwarranted digital hate storms.

10.2. The Infiltration of Bots: 2016 U.S Presidential Elections

The 2016 U.S. Presidential Elections were a watershed, not only in terms of the political landscape but also in defining the role of social media. Following the election, subsequent investigations pointed to Russia's systematic deployment of troll accounts and bots on platforms including Facebook and Twitter, with the intent of manipulating public sentiment and seeding discord.

These social media accounts, posing as everyday Americans, pushed divisive and inflammatory content, further polarizing an already divided electorate and essentially skewing the democratic process. The case underscores the complexity and considerable impact of collective digital behavior in shaping real-world phenomena and, more importantly, the existential threat disinformation poses to the very foundation of societal trust and democratic institutions.

10.3. Push and Pull of Algorithmic Bias - YouTube

YouTube's algorithm has faced long-standing scrutiny for its role in amplifying divisive content. Investigative reports and academic studies have pointed out that YouTube's recommendation system, which is designed to increase viewership, may often lead users down a rabbit hole of progressively extremist content.

Whether we are speaking of political extremism or harmful health misinformation, the algorithm's apparent bias towards sensational and polarizing content underscores the ethical challenges posed by artificial intelligence in tailoring content. The gravity of inadvertent misinformation amplification by such algorithms prompts us to reconsider our framework of accountability and transparency within the digital space.

10.4. The Strength of Collective Policing: Reddit and the Sunil Tripathi Case

In the aftermath of the 2013 Boston Marathon bombing, Reddit turned into an impromptu investigation site. Users began speculating and, in a tragic turn of events, falsely accused missing Brown University student Sunil Tripathi as a potential suspect based on grainy surveillance footage, igniting a firestorm of online vitriol against him.

This instance is a prime example of crowdsourcing gone awry, illustrating the potential hazard of digital collectives bypassing conventional investigatory norms, based solely on conjectures. However, it also brought the prowess of community policing to the fore, as many other Reddit users condemned the speculation and took active measures to eliminate such content from the platform. This renders a glimpse into the potential of social media communities imparting self-governing actions to ensure digitally ethical conduct.

In this journey through key noteworthy cases, we have trawled through the muddy waters of misinformation, digital bias, and community-led actions within the vast planes of social media. While cautionary, these case studies also illuminate the latent potential of humanity's digital expressions: the strength of online communities that shape, influence, and occasionally, rectify errors within the digital sphere. As we venture forth, navigating the limits and possibilities of technological advancements, it is incumbent upon us to tread mindfully, to question, and to actively participate in ensuring transparency, accountability, and ultimately, the validation of truth in our collective narratives in the age of social media. Let us then continue to build and evolve, fostering digital resilience and empowering ourselves with informed perspectives in this ever-unfolding tale of truth and untruth.

Chapter 11. Looking Forward: Safeguarding Truth for Future Generations

In the nuclear age of digital information dissemination, the responsibility we collectively bear to fortify truth is immense. The navigator who charts the tricky waters of a vast digital sea must be versed in the art and science of discerning truth. In this essential final chapter of our expansive exploration, we will reflect on the future, gazing into the crystal ball of technological advancement and societal trends to unravel how we might safeguard truth for the future generations.

11.1. The Importance of Digital Literacy

Digital literacy envisages more than the simple ability to use technology. It encapsulates the skills to locate, understand, assess, create, and communicate using digital technology – skills fully embedded and magnified in the age of social media. Recognizing its paramount importance, educational systems globally are adapting curriculums and methodologies to foster a digitally literate society. For future generations to stand stalwart against misinformation, they must be adequately trained in the art of digital discernment. These are the knights of the keyboard, the champions of truth in our digital age.

11.2. Embracing Fact-Checking

Fact-checking has established itself as a linchpin in our search for authenticity in online information. An array of excellent fact-checking tools and platforms have sprouted in recent years, showcasing innovative ways to verify information. Yet, despite these resources, an alarming number of people fail to do a basic cross-examination of the information they receive. Future generations ought to embrace these tools as their shield against untruths, deploying them with vigilance and constancy.

11.3. The Power of Artificial Intelligence (AI)

Artificial intelligence brings a new dawn in the quest for truth. Already, AI plays a critical role in filtering content, spotting manipulated digital content, and identifying fake accounts. As technology innovates, artificial intelligence will augment our efforts to safeguard truth. It is plausible to anticipate a world where AI systems would be potent enough to autonomously detect and limit misinformation.

11.4. Nudging Ethical Tech Development

One area where the future seems particularly fraught with challenges and opportunities alike is the development of technology. As tech companies become increasingly influential in our lives, there is an acute need for discussions on ethical technology development. It will be a multidimensional endeavor, striving to infuse the values of truth, transparency, and accountability into the technological architecture that permeates our lives.

11.5. Policy Measures

Misinformation is not just a technological issue, but a socio-political one as well. Stricter policy measures, legislation, and international cooperation are required to tackle its spread across national borders. With insights from our lessons and case studies, lawmakers' role in shaping a future where truth is inviolate becomes undeniably clear. They must inhabit the mantle of guardians, protecting our societies from the waves of untruth that threaten to swamp our digital shores.

11.6. Conclusion – Passing Baton to Future Generations

As we conclude our journey in this sprawling digital landscape, we entrust the baton of truth to the future generations. They have a world to win, where truth will not merely survive but thrive, pushing back the fog of misinformation with the sharp beams of knowledge, discernment, and critical thinking. Posterity will undoubtedly face challenges we can only vaguely glimpse today, yet armed with the lessons, insights, and tools we have explored in this comprehensive study, we can help them shape a future underpinned by truth and authenticity.

Endowed with these measures and insights, the search for truth will evolve, but its essence remains unscathed. Let this be our guiding motto: In the digital age, where untruths lurk under the guise of knowledge, nothing reveals truth like knowledge does. What has been charted in our expedition so far is hardly the final destination. It is merely the beginning of our collective quest for truth, signposting the path for future generations as technology hurtles us into the incognito of the future.

This steadfast pursuit of truth in today's social media landscape, as daunting and complex as it may seem, is not just a necessity but our collective responsibility. While misinformation seems to be always a step ahead, our resilience, guided by knowledge and critical thinking, can turn the tide. In the end, the safeguarding of truth doesn't hinge upon our ability to stop misinformation completely, but on our collective strength to challenge it, scrutinize it, and ultimately limit its influence on our shared knowledge pool. It is in this spirit that we must look towards safeguarding truth for future generations, shaping the digital legacy for centuries to come.